Fact Finders®

IMMIGRATION
★ TODAY

# IMMIGRANTS

## ⫷ FROM ⫸

# MEXICO

## ⫷ AND ⫸

# CENTRAL
# AMERICA

BY EMMA CARLSON BERNE

CONSULTANTS:
EMIR ESTRADA, PHD
ASSISTANT PROFESSOR
OF SOCIOLOGY
ARIZONA STATE UNIVERSITY

MIRIAM E. DOWNEY, MLS
CHILDREN'S LIBRARIAN
IMMIGRATION EQUALITY ADVOCATE

CAPSTONE PRESS
a capstone imprint

T0069632

Fact Finders Books are published by Capstone Press,
1710 Roe Crest Drive, North Mankato, Minnesota 56003
www.mycapstone.com

Cataloging-in-publication information is on file with the Library of Congress.
978-1-5435-1383-7 (library binding)
978-1-5435-1387-5 (paperback)
978-1-5435-1399-8 (ebook PDF)

Summary: Gives an overview of the modern immigrant experience in today's uncertain world. By following
three families through their immigration experiences, this book offers first-hand accounts of why they left their
home countries and what they're seeking in the United States. Easy-to-understand language and dynamic
graphics help explain this often contentious issue that's a hot topic in today's media.

Editorial Credits
Editor: Jennifer Huston
Production Artist: Kazuko Collins
Designer: Russell Griesmer
Media Researcher: Eric Gohl
Production specialist: Laura Manthe

Photo Credits: AP Photo: ICE/Bryan Cox, 22, Jose Luis Magana, 26; Getty Images: David McNew, 5, John
Moore, 15, 16, 21, Kris Timken, 25, Omar Torres, 24, Per-Anders Pettersson, 12, PhotoQuest, 11, Spencer Platt, 7;
Newscom: EFE/Alex Segura, 27, KRT/Fernando Salazar, 9, Splash News/AdMedia, 19, ZUMA Press/
Jerry Lara, 17; Shutterstock: bioraven, throughout (passport stamps background), Christopher Penler, 29,
Christos Georghiou, 20, dikobraziy, cover (background), 1, mdurson, cover, Nuangthong, 18, Pyty, 4;
Wikimedia: Daniel J Simanek, 13

Design Elements: Shutterstock

Printed in the United States       5547

# TABLE OF CONTENTS

# CHAPTER 1

# LEAVING THEIR NATIVE LAND

   Mexico and the countries in Central America are vibrant lands. They are full of deserts, rain forests, mountains, banana and coffee farms, and rich **cultures**. Yet, every year, thousands of people choose to leave these countries. For some, it's a difficult decision. They pack their belongings for a long journey to the United States.

   Some, especially those who can afford it, arrive in cars or by airplane. They make their way through checkpoints and present their **visas**. But the experience of many **immigrants** from Mexico and Central America is very different, especially if they are poor. Some have to walk hundreds of miles because they can't afford other forms of transportation. Many face violence, extreme heat, or even death as they try to make it to the United States.

## WAYS TO CROSS THE BORDER

There are two ways to cross the U.S. border legally. You can either drive through a checkpoint or land at an airport and have your ID and visa inspected by **border patrol agents**.

People often cross the border illegally because they don't have visas or other documents to allow them to do so legally, with the proper papers. To avoid border patrol agents, some walk across in places where there is no checkpoint. Some cross in boats. Others pay truck drivers to hide in the back of their large trucks. The truck driver presents his or her papers and crosses legally. Once in the United States, the truck driver lets the people out. But many people die from heat and lack of air in the backs of these trucks.

Each year, nearly 32 million people enter the United States at this border crossing linking Tijuana, Mexico, and San Diego, California.

**culture**—a group of people's beliefs, customs, and way of life
**visa**—a government document giving a person permission to enter a foreign country
**immigrant**—a person who moves from one country to live permanently in another
**border patrol agent**—a member of a law enforcement group that watches over a country's borders

Why would anyone choose to make such a dangerous journey? Violence and poverty affect many people living in Mexico and Central America. Most immigrants from these countries are looking for better, safer lives. Violent gangs have terrorized people in Central America for decades, especially in El Salvador, Honduras, and Guatemala. Families often have to decide between having their lives threatened by gangs and fleeing their homeland.

Poverty adds to the desperate situations a lot of people in Mexico and Central America face. Many cannot find work to support their families. Some of the jobs pay less than $2 a day. This is especially true for people who do not have a formal education or degree. Others farm small pieces of land to grow just enough food to feed their families. But recently the worst **drought** in decades destroyed crops that farmers in Central America were depending on.

**drought**—a long period of weather with little or no rainfall

A young girl stands outside the shack where her family lives in a poor area of Honduras. To make money, her family sells recyclables and other items they find in a nearby dumpster.

# ★ TYPES OF IMMIGRATION ★

A person can be a documented or an **undocumented** immigrant. Most countries, including the United States, have laws saying how many people can move there each year. By law, those who plan to move to the United States must first apply to the U.S. government for a visa. They need to say why they want to move and list any skills and education they have. Once they receive a visa from the U.S. government, they can live in the United States for a certain amount of time. The amount of time varies depending on the type of visa they have. In order to stay, they must apply to become a permanent resident or "green card" holder. They may also apply to become a U.S. citizen. The application process can take many years.

Undocumented immigrants are those who entered the country without visas. They may have walked or driven into the United States without border patrol agents noticing them. Others may have entered the country with a **temporary** visa, but they stayed after it **expired**.

> **undocumented**—without the proper government documents required for legal immigration or residence
> **temporary**—lasting only a short period of time
> **expire**—to come to an end; to no longer be in force

## Traveling with Coyotes

People who enter the United States without a visa often travel with the help of guides called "coyotes." Coyotes guide people through Central America and Mexico and across the U.S. border—for a fee of thousands of dollars. Sometimes they take the money and then abandon the people on the journey. Coyotes often threaten the immigrants with violence if they don't do what the coyotes say.

Led by a "coyote," a group of undocumented immigrants attempts to cross into the United States.

About 26 percent of all immigrants living in the United States are undocumented. About half of them are from Mexico. Why are so many immigrants from this country undocumented? Most immigrants from this area would prefer to enter the country with the proper documents. As of 2018, there were nearly 1.3 million Mexicans waiting for a visa to immigrate to the United States. In some cases, it can take more than 20 years to receive an immigration visa. This is because no country can receive more than 1,793 (7 percent) of the 25,620 immigration visas available each year. The demand for immigration visas is far greater in some countries, such as Mexico, than the number available.

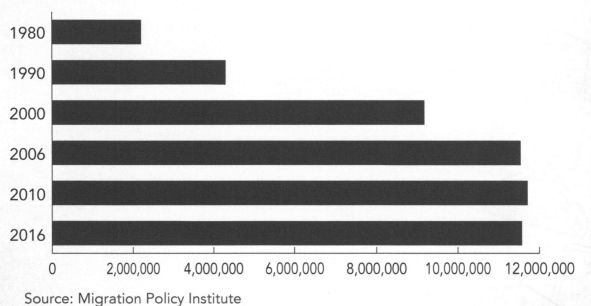

NUMBER OF MEXICAN IMMIGRANTS
IN THE UNITED STATES, 1980–2016

Source: Migration Policy Institute

# MEXICAN IMMIGRANTS IN THE UNITED STATES

Mexican people have been moving to the United States since the mid-1800s. At first they came to the United States to work on farms and then returned home. The most famous example of this was the Bracero program, which began in 1942. This program allowed millions of Mexican laborers to be hired for work on farms when the U.S. was experiencing a shortage of agriculture workers during World War II. Many workers stayed in the United States after the program ended and encouraged their family and friends to join them.

The Mexican immigrant population in the United States has increased greatly since the 1980s. This is due to political unrest and worker shortages in America. However, since 2006, it has remained relatively flat and has actually decreased slightly in the last few years. This decrease is due to stronger border patrols, a weaker U.S. economy, and fewer job opportunities in the United States.

Farm workers from Mexico register for the Bracero program.

# CHAPTER 2

# THREE IMMIGRATION STORIES

Dulce Garcia came to the United States as a child. Dulce doesn't remember much about Mexico. She was only 4 years old when her family left in the late 1980s. They crossed the border into the United States illegally, without documents from the U.S. government, and made their way to San Diego, California.

Dulce's family had been very poor in Mexico. In the United States, they were still very poor and often didn't get enough to eat. They also struggled with homelessness at times. Sometimes they could only afford to rent one room in a house, and they often slept on the floor.

Some families make the difficult decision to leave their home countries for better opportunities for their children. Young children make the long journey with their parents, often on foot.

Miguel Sanchez had a very different experience as an immigrant from Mexico. Miguel was born in 1970 to middle-class parents. His family lived in a nice home in the city of Puebla. In 1981 Miguel's father received a student visa to study for a PhD at the University of Wisconsin in Madison.

In Madison, Miguel's family lived on a college campus full of people from all over the world. Miguel learned English quickly and was easily accepted into American school culture. In fact, by the time he

Winters in Wisconsin are quite different than in Mexico, but Miguel Sanchez came to feel at home in America.

was a teenager, Miguel felt more American than Mexican. When his father finished his studies and the family returned to Mexico, Miguel felt out of place. At his high school in Puebla, he felt like an outsider.

# FLEEING VIOLENCE AND POVERTY

Ruby's story is different from both Dulce's and Miguel's. Ruby didn't have the protection of her parents when she left Honduras with her sister Maira at age 15. Ana, Ruby's older sister, lived in the United States cleaning houses for a living. Ruby, Maira, and their mother relied on money that Ana sent home.

There is a lot of gang violence in Honduras, and Ruby could sense that there was no future for her there. She had no way of getting an education or a job. So in the fall of 2013, Ruby, Maira, and three other family members left Honduras. They walked from Honduras through Guatemala and into Mexico. But Mexican authorities discovered Ruby's group and sent them back to Honduras. They ended up right back where they had started.

In Honduras, 60 percent of the population lives in poverty, meaning that they are very poor. In some areas, many people live on less than $2 per day.

But Ruby was determined to try again. Soon, she left with Maira and their family members. They walked and got rides from strangers, and this time, they made it to the U.S. border. They had traveled 1,600 miles (2,575 kilometers). However, they still needed to cross the Rio Grande—the large river that divides Mexico and the United States. If they could get across the river, they would be in the United States.

Some people offered to take Ruby and her group to the other side in their boat. The girls climbed in, and the boat drove to the other side of the river. They had made it to the United States.

## UNACCOMPANIED CHILD IMMIGRANTS

In recent years an increased number of children have left Mexico and Central America without their parents or other adults. Many parents send their children to the United States to escape extreme violence in their home countries. For families wanting to get their children to a safer place, coyotes are one of the few options.

A border patrol agent speaks to some children who were caught crossing the border without the proper documents.

But the people in the boat would not let them go. They took Ruby and her family members to a house in Texas. Then they forced Ruby to call her sister Ana and tell her to send money in order to release them.

Like the people shown here, Ruby and her family members were helped across the Rio Grande in a boat.

# LIFE IN THE UNITED STATES

Miguel's years as a teenager in the United States had a major impact on his life. He spoke both English and Spanish and was familiar with American culture. After graduating from college in Mexico, he worked for a bank there. When Miguel was offered a job with a software company in California, he took it. His company helped him apply for an H1B visa, which is only for skilled workers. In April 1995 Miguel moved to California and began work.

By the time Miguel was 27, he was married and had a small child. He started to think about officially becoming an American citizen. But first he needed permanent resident status, also called a green card. Miguel received his green card in 2000, five years after moving to California.

A green card allows a person born in another country to permanently live and work in the United States.

Miguel had to wait another five years after getting his green card to apply for citizenship. He applied in late 2005, and just a few months later, he was a U.S. citizen. Becoming a U.S. citizen was meaningful to Miguel. But not because he was becoming an American—he'd already felt like one for many years. It was meaningful because he had the full rights and protections of an American citizen.

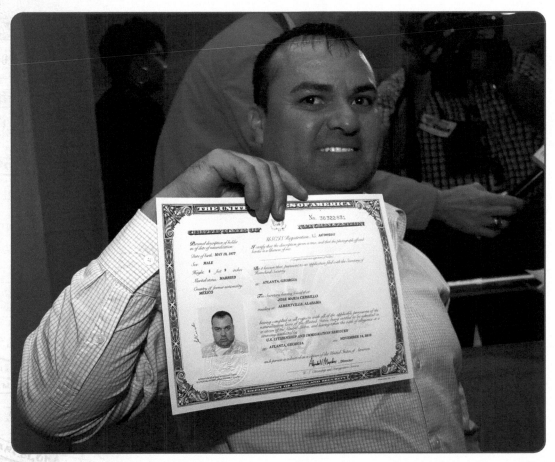

Mexican-born Jose Cerrillo shows the certificate he received after becoming a legal American citizen.

# THE PATH TO U.S. CITIZENSHIP

The path for becoming a U.S. citizen can be long, confusing, and difficult. Adult immigrants must fill out many applications, be interviewed, and take tests. Eventually they swear their loyalty to the United States in a special ceremony. Parents complete this paperwork for their children under age 18. Those children become U.S. citizens when their parents do.

Adult immigrants must be at least 18 years old before applying to become a U.S. citizen.

When applying for citizenship, the immigrant must have been a legal permanent resident (green card holder) for at least 5 years.

The applicant must "be a person of good moral character," according to the U.S. government.

The applicant must pass a citizenship test that shows a basic understanding of U.S. history and laws and the English language.

The immigrant must take an oath of allegiance to the United States, and then receives a certificate making him or her a U.S. citizen.

Source: USA.gov

Ruby's first experience in the United States was very different from Miguel's. She and her family members spent their first days in the United States held against their will. After two weeks, they got away and called for help.

Like Ruby, this young woman and child were stopped by border patrol agents.

The help came in the form of border patrol agents. Ruby and the others had been caught entering the United States without the proper documents from the government. But Ruby wasn't deported because she was under 18 years old. Children under 18 who are caught living in the United States without parents and the proper documents are protected to some degree. They can still be deported, but it takes longer. It wasn't a permanent fix, but Ruby was allowed to stay.

Like Ruby, Dulce Garcia's parents were terrified of being deported. Unlike Ruby, Dulce's parents were adults, and there were no laws protecting their stay or rights. Dulce's mother and father were afraid they would be caught if they left their home. "We felt scared . . . to step outside our house, even to go to the movies. . .," Dulce remembered.

Immigration and Customs Enforcement (ICE) officers surround a home where they believe undocumented immigrants may be living. If caught, undocumented immigrants may be forced to return to their home countries.

The fear and uncertainty that Dulce experienced is typical for undocumented immigrants living in the United States. Undocumented immigrants have a right to fair and equal treatment, but the right often goes unprotected. They have few legal rights and no official status as citizens. Immigration and Customs Enforcement—the government body known as ICE—can arrest them at any time. If that happens, they can be put in jail or deported. Some people were brought to the United States as babies or young children. They have spent most of their lives in the United States before getting deported. Life in the United States is all they have ever known. They feel more connected to American culture than that of their homeland. When forced to return to their native countries, they sometimes feel like outsiders.

## DID YOU KNOW?

To work legally in the United States, an immigrant needs a work visa, which undocumented immigrants do not have. Without a work visa, they would have to find an employer who is willing to hire undocumented immigrants.

# CHAPTER 4

# THE FUTURE OF IMMIGRATION

About one in seven people living in the United States was born a citizen of another country. Of these immigrants, 26.5 percent are from Mexico. In 2016 more than 43.7 million immigrants (both documented and undocumented) were living in the United States. That's 13.5 percent of the nation's population.

As of 2016, there were 11.6 million people living in the United States who were born in Mexico.

**prejudice**—hatred or dislike of people who belong to a certain social group, such as a race or religion
**discrimination**—treating people unfairly because of their race, country of birth, or gender

Many immigrants often face **prejudice**, **discrimination**, and are the victims of hate crimes. Some people think that all immigrants from Mexico and Central America are undocumented. Many also believe immigrants are taking jobs away from Americans. This anti-immigrant prejudice is not new in the United States. Italian, Irish, Chinese, Indian, and Jewish immigrants have all suffered discrimination.

Miguel Sanchez and his family were lucky. They felt accepted in the United States. They made friends at school, work, and in the community.

Many immigrants from Mexico and Central America have felt welcomed in the United States.

# ★ DREAMERS IN AMERICA ★

In 2012 President Barack Obama approved a program known as DACA (Deferred Action for Childhood Arrival). According to DACA, undocumented people who came to the United States as children could legally live and work in the country. The people the DACA program helps are referred to as DREAMers (Development, Relief and Education for Alien Minors). There are approximately 800,000 DREAMers in the United States. Most of them cannot remember living in the country where they were born. The United States is the only home they've ever known.

Young DREAMers fill out papers to live and work legally in the United States through the DACA program.

Thousands of people protested Trump's proposed ending of the DACA program.

During Donald Trump's campaign for president, he promised to stop illegal immigration. He also promised to end the DACA program. In September 2017 President Trump kept his promise and announced that he was ending DACA.

Dulce Garcia is a DREAMer, but she's no longer the scared girl she was growing up. She is now a lawyer, and she is fighting for herself and the other DREAMers. Dulce and others, including several states, are challenging the end to DACA and changes to other laws that negatively affect immigrants. They believe the Trump administration did not have the legal right to end DACA. "For me, this lawsuit means having a voice for [the DREAMers]," Dulce said. "We're speaking on our own behalf."

The number of people that Dulce speaks for will continue to grow. The immigrant population is on the rise and shows no sign of stopping. Ruby is part of that population. She has avoided being sent back to Honduras for now. Ruby eventually joined her sister Ana in Maryland. Ana is helping Ruby stay in the United States with the hope of becoming an American citizen. Ruby even has a lawyer to speak up for her in court.

The United States has long been a country made up of immigrants. Except those whose ancestors are Native Americans, most Americans have relatives who were once immigrants to the United States. But U.S. citizens have always argued over who is allowed to immigrate and become citizens and who is not. Mexican and Central American immigrants in the 21st century are now part of that historic debate. And their goals are basically the same as those of other immigrants of the past 300 years. They want to work hard and have better lives for themselves and their families than they could in their home countries.

**DID YOU KNOW?**

In 1910 most of America's immigrant population was born in Germany. In 2016 Mexico was the top country of origin for immigrants in the United States.

# GLOSSARY

**border patrol agent** (BOR-dur puh-TROHL AY-juhnt)—a member of a law enforcement group that watches over a country's borders

**culture** (KUHL-chur)—a group of people's beliefs, customs, and way of life

**discrimination** (dis-kri-muh-NAY-shuhn)—treating people unfairly because of their race, country of birth, or gender

**drought** (DROUT)—a long period of weather with little or no rainfall

**expire** (ek-SPIRE)—to come to an end; to no longer be in force

**immigrant** (IM-i-gruhnt)—a person who moves from one country to live permanently in another

**prejudice** (PREJ-uh-diss)—hatred or dislike of people who belong to a certain social group, such as a race or religion

**temporary** (TEM-puh-rair-ee)—lasting only a short period of time

**undocumented** (un-DAHK-yoo-men-ted)—without the proper government documents required for legal immigration or residence

**visa** (VEE-zuh)—a government document giving a person permission to enter a foreign country

## READ MORE

**Barghoorn, Linda**. *A Refugee's Journey from El Salvador.* Leaving My Homeland. New York: Crabtree Publishing, 2018.

**Henzel, Cynthia Kennedy**. *Mexican Immigrants: In Their Shoes.* Mankato, Minn.: Child's World, 2017.

**MacCarald, Clara**. *Becoming an American Citizen.* American Citizenship. Minneapolis, Minn.: Core Library, 2017.

## INTERNET SITES

Use FactHound to find Internet sites related to this book.

Visit www.facthound.com

Just type in 9781543513837 and go.

## CRITICAL THINKING QUESTIONS

1. What are three reasons people choose to immigrate to the United States? What is one common factor among all three? Use details from the text to support your answer.

2. Review the infographic on page 10. Using your knowledge and details from the text, why do you think the Mexican immigrant population in the United States steadily increased until the mid-2000s but has been relatively flat in recent years?

3. Choose two of the immigration experiences discussed in Chapter 3 to compare and contrast. How are the stories of these immigrants similar? How are they different?

# INDEX